Early Foundations in the Bible

Jesus

God's Son Is Born

John and Kim Walton
Illustrated by Alice Craig

The Early Foundations in the Bible Series . . .

- Moses and the Mighty Plagues
- Jonah and the Big Fish
- God and the World He Made
- Elijah and the Contest
- Daniel and the Lions
- Abraham and His Big Family
- Jesus, God's Son Is Born
- Paul and the Bright Light
- Samuel and the Voice in the Night
- Adam and Eve in the Garden
- David Fights Goliath
- Jeroboam and the Golden Calves
- Noah and the Flood
- Esther the Queen

Chariot Books™ is an imprint of David C. Cook Publishing Co.
David C. Cook Publishing Co., Elgin, Illinois 60120
David C. Cook Publishing Co., Weston, Ontario

JESUS: GOD'S SON IS BORN

Based on Matthew 2 and Luke 2

First printing, 1987; Second printing, 1989
Printed in the United States of America
93 92 91 90 89 6 5 4 3 2
ISBN 1-55513-230-8
LC 87-70612

A Word to Parents

As a Bible professor, I find that too much of my time is spent "unteaching"—trying to reverse incorrect notions that students have picked up along the way from children's storybooks or well-meaning Sunday school materials. Naturally we simplify stories for children; they can hardly be expected to grasp all that is involved in Scripture, or even understand all the words. But early exposure to Bible stories, correctly interpreted and applied, provides a good basis for later learning.

The Early Foundations in the Bible series is committed to the authority of the biblical text. The illustrations, brightly colored and two dimensional, are historically and biblically accurate, as far as the detail allows. The interpretation of some stories may differ a little from that with which you're familiar; the notes on the last page of each book explain the biblical basis for the story. These notes, while far more detailed than your preschooler needs, will help you understand the background of the story and answer questions your child might have.

We pray that your child will enjoy these stories and grow up well versed in God's Word.

John H. Walton

Mary and Joseph were about to have a baby.

An angel told them their baby would be the Son of God.

Just before the baby came, Mary and Joseph had to take a trip to Bethlehem.

When they got to Bethlehem, they couldn't find any place to stay.

Finally they found a stable—and that's where the baby was born!

Mary and Joseph named him Jesus.

Angels spread
the news of this special
baby—God's Son.

Shepherds heard about it from the angels and ran to see the baby Jesus.

They worshipped Him.

Even the stars
spread the news in
their own way.

Wise Men far away saw a special star.

They knew that a King had been born—Jesus!

The Wise Men brought gifts to honor Him.

God born as a baby boy! This was the most important thing that had ever happened . . .

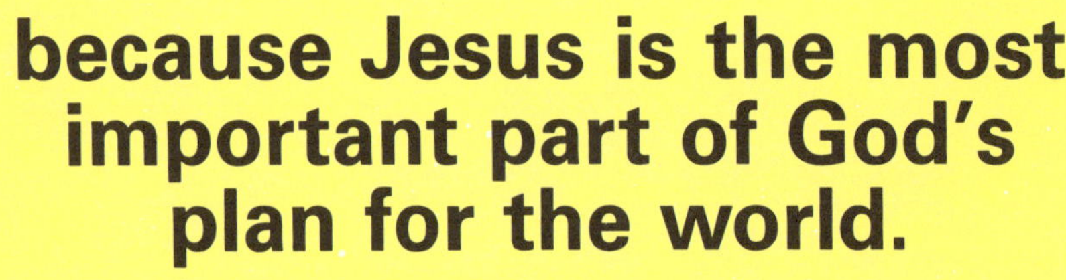

because Jesus is the most important part of God's plan for the world.

Did You Realize . . .

(These notes from the author are for you the parent, offering further explanation and interpretation of the text. While much of the information is far beyond what your preschooler could understand, it can equip you to answer questions that your child might raise.)

Page 4

Mary and Joseph were required to go to Bethlehem, the city of their ancestors, in order to participate in a Roman census for tax purposes.

Page 10

There is some evidence that the stable was a cave rather than a freestanding structure. If it was freestanding, it most likely would have been constructed of mud brick as most buildings in Palestine were.

Page 22

These Wise Men were called Magi. The Magi were priests of Zoroastrianism in the area of present-day Iran. As early as two centuries before the birth of Christ, prophecies circulated among the Magi of a Great King or an incarnate Savior whose birth would be announced by the appearance of a special star. The prophecies speak variously of a bright star that outshines the sun, a falling star, and a star that is at the top of a great column of fire pointing to the place of the birth. Whether the Magi who came to see Jesus had seen something this magnificent, or whether they simply saw an unfamiliar heavenly body and followed its movements, is not clarified in the text of Matthew. Here the star is shown at first as something that only skilled astrologers would recognize as different. Then the column of light that the Magi expected showed them the exact location.

Page 24

By the time the Magi find Jesus, the family is living in a house.

Page 26

The gifts—gold, frankincense, and myrrh—were all of considerable value. Both frankincense and myrrh are fragrant spices native only to the South Arabian area. Frankincense was used in sacrifices of worship and as a medicine. Myrrh was more often used as a perfume, but it also had a medicinal use. Both were used as burial spices. In Roman times one pound of frankincense cost more than two weeks' average wages. A camel could carry 300-400 pounds of frankincense—the equivalent of three or four years' income.

Page 30

God's plan for the world is to provide a way that people can be reconciled to God. Sending Jesus, His own Son, was God's way of bringing us back to Himself. Jesus was sent to die in our place to pay for our sin. If we accept His payment on our behalf, our sins can be forgiven. We hope that this book will provide an opportunity to explain this simply to children. Even though most children of the age that will be using these books cannot understand or make this kind of decision as yet, they can begin to hear the language and get used to the ideas.